THE
IRISH
ACTORS'
QUOTATION BOOK

THE
IRISH
ACTORS'
QUOTATION BOOK

Compiled by Andrew Russell

SOMERVILLE PRESS

Somerville Press Ltd,
Dromore, Bantry, Co. Cork, Ireland

©Andrew Russell 2017
First published 2017

Typeset in Minion Pro

ISBN: 978 0 9955239 68

Printed and bound in Spain
by Graphy Cems, Villatuerta, Navarra

Front cover: Barry Fitgerald, Maureen O'Hara,
Dermot Morgan, and Peter O'Toole

INTRODUCTION

As a land of storytellers, Ireland has also been naturally home to a host of great actors. In *The Irish Actors' Quotation Book,* those who have made their mark on stage and screen over the past century, both domestically and internationally, share their thoughts on life, on themselves, and on the ups and downs and ins and outs of their profession.

OLD AGE DOESN'T CREEP UP ON
YOU, IT COMES RIGHT UP BEHIND
YOU AND SLAPS YOU ON THE
BACK AND IT SAYS 'HOWYA'.

Jim Bartley

I BECAME A MINISTER OF THE
EUCHARIST WHEN I WAS 17. MY
PARENTS AREN'T VERY STRICT
CATHOLICS, BUT FOR SOME
REASON I DECIDED THIS IS WHAT
I WANT TO DO, AND I HAVE KEPT
IT UP.

Sarah Bolger

I HAD TO HAVE SOME BALLS TO
BE IRISH CATHOLIC IN SOUTH
LONDON. MOST OF THAT TIME I
SPENT FIGHTING.

Pierce Brosnan

I WAS AWARE THAT I WAS NOT
GETTING THE GOOD ACTING
ROLES BECAUSE I WAS EITHER
TOO HANDSOME, TOO PRETTY OR
WHATEVER. I WAS BEING JUDGED
IN WAYS THAT LEFT ME NOWHERE
TO GO. YOU HAVE TO BE PATIENT.

Pierce Brosnan

I THINK THERE'S A BIT OF THE DEVIL IN EVERYBODY. THERE'S A BIT OF A PRIEST IN EVERYBODY, TOO, BUT I ENJOYED PLAYING THE DEVIL MORE. HE WAS MORE FUN.

Gabriel Byrne

It was either Voltaire or Charlie Sheen who said, 'We are born alone. We live alone. We die alone. And anything in between that can give us the illusion that we're not, we cling to.'

Gabriel Byrne

I REMEMBER PRFORMING IN
A SCHOOL OPERETTA AND
THE THOUGHT COMING, 'YOU
WILL NOT BE A DENTIST. YOU
WILL TREAD THE BOARDS AND
POSTURE IN THE SPOTLIGHT'S
BEAM.'

Barry Cassin

A BENEVOPENT HAND WAS
RESTED ON MY SHOULDER
AND I AWAITED THE MASTER'S
WORDS. IN MICHAEL'S [MAC
LIAMMÓIR'S] MOST MELLIFLUOUS
TONES THEY CAME, 'MY DEAR
BARRY, THE CRITICS? FUCK
THEM.'

Barry Cassin

IF YOU ASKED ME FOR MY NEW
YEAR RESOLUTION, IT WOULD BE
TO FIND OUT WHO I AM.

Cyril Cusack

THEY SAY 6 MILLION PEOPLE SEE
YOU WHEN YOU ACT IN A FILM; IT
MAY ONLY BE 600 IN A PLAY. BUT
THE EFFECT ON THE 600 MAY BE
TRUER AND MORE LASTING.

Cyril Cusack

So often I'll feel I haven't got the tools. I haven't got the equipment, I haven't got the understanding. I'll never be able to do it. It's like you're at base camp at Mount Everest looking up, thinking, 'I won't be able to scale that.' But you trudge on.

Sinéad Cusack

I THINK BEING IRISH I POSSIBLY
FIND A CONNECTION WITH
AMERICAN WRITERS AND INDEED
RUSSIAN WRITERS MORE EASILY
THAN I DO WITH ENGLISH
WRITERS BECAUSE IRELAND
AND ENGLAND ARE SO CLOSE
GEOGRAPHICALLY, ONE IS VERY
AWARE OF THE DIFFERENCES.

Sorcha Cusack

I SUPPOSE I HAVE A HIGHLY
DEVELOPED CAPACITY FOR SELF-
DELUSION, SO IT'S NO PROBLEM
FOR ME TO BELIEVE THAT I'M
SOMEBODY ELSE.

Daniel Day-Lewis

IF YOU HAVE A CERTAIN
WILDNESS OF SPIRIT, A CABINET
MAKER'S WORKSHOP IS NOT THE
PLACE TO EXPRESS IT.

Daniel Day-Lewis

I LIKE PLAYING CHARACTERS
WHO ARE FRACTURED, BROKEN.
I FIND THAT MORE RELATABLE,
FOR SOME REASON. I DON'T FEEL
THAT I'M LIKE THAT MYSELF
BY NATURE, BUT THERE'S JUST
SOMETHING THAT YOU CAN
REALLY GRAB HOLD OF IF PEOPLE
HAVE A DARKNESS IN THEM, I
THINK.

Jamie Dornan

I DON'T CARE ABOUT
NATIONALISM, I CARE ABOUT THE
THEATRE.

Hilton Edwards

PAIN SEEMS TO BE EASIER,
OR MELANCHOLY SEEMS TO
BE EASIER TO PORTRAY IN A
CHARACTER. I DON'T KNOW IF
THAT'S BECAUSE I'M A HUMAN
BEING OR BECAUSE I'M AN
IRISHMAN OR BOTH.

Colin Farrell

I'M ALWAYS INTERESTED IN
TRYING TO INVESTIGATE
DIFFERENT PERSONALITIES. I
WANT TO KEEP MYSELF GUESSING
AND KEEP THE FEAR ELEMENT
ALIVE, SO THAT I DON'T GET TOO
COMFORTABLE.

Michael Fassbender

A GOLF COURSE IS NOTHING BUT
A POOLROOM MOVED OUTDOORS

Barry Fitzgerald

I AM PROUD OF MY REBELLIOUS
MOMENTS, BUT I WISH I'D
HANDLED THEM WITH MORE WIT.

Geraldine Fitzgerald

UNTIL I GOT CLEAN I COULDN'T
TAKE CONTROL OF MY LIFE
IN A WAY THAT WAS EITHER
SPIRITUALLY MEANINGFUL OR
HEALTHY. I TALK ABOUT IT
ONLY BECAUSE I THINK THERE
ARE MANY WOMEN OUT THERE
WHO ARE SUFFERING SIMILARLY,
ASHAMED TO SEEK HELP. IT
DOESN'T HAVE TO BE THAT WAY.

Fionnula Flanagan

WHEN I'M LYING DRUNK AT
AN AIRPORT THE PRESS CALL
ME IRISH…BUT WHEN I WIN
AN OSCAR, I'M CLASSIFIED AS
BRITISH.

Brenda Fricker

EVERY PART I PLAY IS JUST
A VARIANT OF MY OWN
PERSONALITY. NO REAL
CHARACTER ACTOR, OF COURSE,
JUST ME.

Michael Gambon

There's no subtext in 'Harry Potter,' really; it's all magic - anything can happen. Why do I say this? Because it's a magic spell. It's quite nice in a way. There is a real freedom to it. Doesn't say much for acting, does it?

Michael Gambon

I HOPE IT'S NOT ALL I'LL EVER
DO, BUT I KNOW I'VE PLAYED
ENIGMATIC CHARACTERS. FOR
ME, THE GOOD CHARACTERS ARE
PEOPLE WHO GET PLACES, ARE
DEVIOUS, ARE CUNNING AND
TRICKY AND HARD TO PIN DOWN.
OBVIOUSLY, IF YOU PLAY ONE
AND YOU DO AN OKAY JOB OF IT,
THAT'LL BE ON PEOPLE'S MINDS.

Aidan Gillen

Everything's borne out of
human experience, of course
- rejection, humiliation,
poverty, whatever.
People aren't born bad,
no matter how harsh the
circumstances. There is a
person in there, and that
person is not made of ice.

Aidan Gillen

I LOVED TEACHING. AND I ALWAYS USED TO SAY THAT ACTING WAS JUST SOMETHING I DID PURELY ON MY OWN TERMS, AND THAT IF I HAD TO MAKE A LIVING FROM IT THERE WOULD BE TOO MUCH PRESSURE.

Brendan Gleeson

I DON'T PLAN IN TERMS OF
CAREER AMBITIONS. THE ONLY
CAREER AMBITION I HAVE IS TO
WORK WITH PEOPLE WHO ARE
GOING TO BRING YOU UP AND
ELEVATE YOUR PERFORMANCE.
THEY'LL LET YOU KNOW THINGS
THAT YOU DIDN'T KNOW
ALREADY AND BRING YOU PLACES
THAT YOU MIGHT NOT HAVE
GOTTEN TO OTHERWISE.

Brendan Gleeson

LIFE IS DIFFICULT FOR EVERYONE;
EVERYONE HAS BAD DAYS.
EVERYONE HAS TROUBLE IN
THEIR LIFE, BECAUSE IT DOESN'T
MATTER HOW RICH YOU ARE:
SICKNESS AND TROUBLE AND
WORRY AND LOVE, THESE THINGS
WILL MESS WITH YOU AT EVERY
LEVEL OF LIFE.

Domhnall Gleeson

POETS SHOULD NEVER MARRY.
THE WORLD SHOULD THANK ME
FOR NOT MARRYING YOU.

Maude Gonne
in a letter to W. B. Yeats

THERE'S MORE FICTION IN MY
LIFE THAN IN BOOKS, SO I DON'T
BOTHER WITH THEM.

Richard Harris

I OFTEN SIT BACK AND THINK, I
WISH I'D DONE THAT, AND FIND
OUT LATER THAT I ALREADY
HAVE.

Richard Harris

I JUST DO IT... AND LET THE
AUDIENCE MAKE UP THEIR OWN
MIND.

Tom Hickey

Grief is exhausting. When you learn – maybe through my age or experience – trying to harness the energy, whatever it is, muted energy or a concentration to find yourself in a place? You try to use it for when it's really necessary and can arrive.

Ciarán Hinds

You try to work with the
director and your fellow
actors to get somewhere,
but other people are the
judge of whether you hit
that note right.

Ciarán Hinds

IT'S THE SAME AS ANY CHARACTER, ANY REAL HUMAN, YOU FIND OUT AS MUCH ABOUT THEM AS YOU POSSIBLY CAN. YOU DON'T HAVE TO BRING IT INTO THE PERFORMANCE. BUT IT IS THERE IN THE BACKGROUND.

Bosco Hogan

I LOVE NOT KNOWING WHAT'S COMING NEXT. IN WAYS, IT'S TERRIFYING, BUT I LOVE HOW DIFFERENT IT IS.

Amy Huberman

DON'T THEY SAY ACTING IS THE
SHY MAN'S REVENGE?

John Kavanagh

I'VE BEEN 52 TO 53 YEARS ON STAGE AND YET 'FAWLTY TOWERS', THOSE FULL NINE MINUTES, MAKE ME RECOGNISED ANYWHERE IN THE WORLD.

David Kelly

IT TOOK ME TWO HOURS TO BE
MADE UP AS FATHER JACK. I
FOUND IT REPULSIVE. IF I WAS IN
COSTUME, NOBODY WOULD SIT
BESIDE ME.

Frank Kelly

THERE WAS NO ACTING IN MY
FAMILY, HOWEVER, I ALWAYS FELT
THAT I WOULD NEVER BE HAPPY
OR FULFILLED DOING ANYTHING
ELSE.

Des Keogh

Drama school taught me to become a bit more of a human being because you can't hate people and be an actor. It doesn't work.

Charlie Lawson

I REMEMBER RUNNING UP TO MY
DAD AND SAYING, 'I WANT TO BE
AN ACTOR WHEN I GROW UP!'
AND HIM SAYING, 'YEAH, WELL,
WE'LL TALK ABOUT IT.'

Allen Leech

OF COURSE I'M VOLATILE.
AREN'T ALL ACTRESSES?

Rosaleen Linehan

I DON'T WANT TO SOUND LIKE A
GRUMPY OLD MAN BUT THERE
ARE STILL PEOPLE OUT THERE,
WHO I WORK WITH, WHO ARE
'REAL ACTORS' AND YOU KNOW
THEM WHEN YOU COME ACROSS
THEM.

John Lynch

WE ARE BORN AT THE RISE OF
THE CURTAIN AND WE DIE WITH
ITS FALL, AND EVERY NIGHT IN
THE PRESENCE OF OUR PATRONS
WE WRITE OUR NEW CREATION,
AND EVERY NIGHT IT IS BLOTTED
OUT FOREVER; AND OF WHAT USE
IS IT TO SAY TO AUDIENCE OR TO
CRITIC, 'AH, BUT YOU SHOULD
HAVE SEEN ME LAST TUESDAY?'

Micheál Mac Liammóir

LIFE IS A LONG REHEARSAL FOR A
PLAY THAT IS NEVER PRODUCED.

Micheál Mac Liammóir

THIS STUFF'S NOT BAD, BUT
ISN'T IT A BIT, YOU KNOW, LIKE
INFLATABLE WOMEN?

Donal McCann
on non-alcoholic beer

IT'S BEEN A GRADUAL, GROWING
THING. LIKE DRINKING TOO
MUCH.

Donal McCann
on being a Roman Catholic

IT'S VERY HARD TO PRACTICE
ACTING. ATHLETES CAN TRAIN,
DANCERS CAN DANCE, PAINTERS
CAN PAINT…ACTORS CAN ONLY
ACT WHEN THEY'RE ACTING.

Barry McGovern

WHEN IT FIRST CAME OUT IT WAS
SO AVANT-GARDE PEOPLE DIDN'T
KNOW WHAT TO MAKE OF IT.
IT WASN'T THE KIND OF WELL-
MADE PLAY THEY WERE USED TO.
THE PROBLEM IS, *WAITING FOR
GODOT* IS LIKE MOZART: TOO
EASY FOR CHILDREN AND TOO
DIFFICULT
FOR ADULTS.

Barry McGovern

I'VE NEVER DONE A
ONE-MAN SHOW. I SHY AWAY
FROM THEM BECAUSE THEY'VE
NOTHING TO DO WITH ACTING.

T. P. McKenna

My old manager of the
Irish National Theatre said
'Don't worry about being
a star, just worry about
being a working actor. Just
keep working.' I think that's
really good advice.

Colm Meaney

I KIND OF HAVE AN INTEREST
IN ALL HISTORY. AND I SUSPECT
IT COMES FROM BEING IRISH
– WE LIKE STORIES, WE LIKE
TELLING STORIES, WHICH MAKES
A LOT OF US LEAN TOWARDS
BEING WRITERS OR ACTORS OR
DIRECTORS.

Colm Meaney

I DON'T BOTHER WITH DRUGS
MYSELF BECAUSE I'M AT THAT
AGE NOW; I DON'T NEED TO. IF I
WANT A RUSH, I JUST GET OUT OF
A CHAIR WHEN I DON'T EXPECT
IT.

Dylan Moran

I THINK THAT WOMEN JUST HAVE A PRIMEVAL INSTINCT TO MAKE SOUP, WHICH THEY WILL TRY TO FOIST ON ANYBODY WHO LOOKS LIKE A LIKELY CANDIDATE.

Dylan Moran

WHEN INVOLVED WITH FILMING,
THE THOUGHT COMES FINALLY
INTO FOCUS: I WONDER WHAT
THE GROWN-UPS ARE DOING.

Dermot Morgan

I SUPPOSE I WAS GETTING TO
BE WHAT THEY CALL A JOKER,
AND I'M NOT SURE I LIKE WHAT
THAT IS IF YOU'RE NOT DOING IT
PROFESSIONALLY...

Dermot Morgan

I ASKED ANN WOULD SHE
CONSIDER BECOMING MY SECOND
WIFE. I QUICKLY EXPLAINED THE
THEATRE WAS MY FIRST WIFE.

Eamon Morrissey

THEN I WANTED THE CHARACTER
TO BE FEMININE AS OPPOSED TO
EFFEMINATE. BECAUSE IT'S EASY
TO BE CAMP OR QUEEN. ANYONE
CAN DO THAT. WHAT'S DIFFICULT
IS TO PLAY FEMININE.

Cillian Murphy

My wife can see always how
a part affects me personally
because she has to live with
it.

Cillian Murphy

SOME MORNINGS YOU WAKE
UP AND THINK, GEE I LOOK
HANDSOME TODAY. OTHER DAYS I
THINK, WHAT AM I DOING IN THE
MOVIES? I WANNA GO BACK TO
IRELAND AND DRIVE A FORKLIFT.

Liam Neeson

ACTING IS INVIGORATING. BUT
I DON'T ANALYSE IT TOO MUCH.
IT'S LIKE A DOG SMELLING
WHERE IT'S GOING TO DO ITS
TOILET IN THE MORNING.

Liam Neeson

In Los Angeles, it's like they jog for two hours a day and then they think they're morally right. That's when you want to choke people, you know?

Liam Neeson

YOU DON'T COME TO SEE A
GREEK PLAY AND NOT WANT
BLOOD AND GORE AND DEPTH OF
FEELING FROM YOUR BOOTS UP.

Ruth Negga

WHAT WOULD YOU DO IF I WEREN'T AN ACTOR? I WOULD BE SOMEBODY DESPERATELY TRYING TO BE AN ACTOR.

Jim Norton

I GREW UP AMONG STRONG
WOMEN SO I KNOW WHAT
IT'S LIKE TO BE LOVED AND
HUMILIATED IN A HEARTBEAT.

Chris O'Dowd

I THINK I'M GOING TO KEEP MY
IRISH ACCENT FOREVER NOW IN
ANY MOVIE I MAKE, BECAUSE
CHICKS DIG IT AND THAT'S ALL I
CARE ABOUT NOW!

Chris O'Dowd

HOW COULD YOU HAVE HAD
SUCH A WONDERFUL LIFE AS
ME IF THERE WASN'T A GOD
DIRECTING?

Maureen O'Hara

Escapism should be the central core of movies. I get bored with realistic films, even when they are well done.

Dan O'Herlihy

AN ACTOR IS ALMOST A
SHEPHERD, AND HE HAS THIS
HERD OF GOATS, AND SOMETIMES
THERE ARE A FEW STRAYS THAT
WANDER, AND YOU PUT THEM IN
THIS PEN, AND THEN TAKE THEM
OUT AND PUT THEM IN ANOTHER
PEN. YOU'RE GETTING THEM ALL
TO LAUGH AT THE SAME TIME, TO
GET A SENSE OF YOUR RHYTHM
OF DELIVERY.

Milo O'Shea

I SEEM TO HAVE A ONE-TRACK
MIND. WHEN I WAS HAVING
BABIES, I DID NOTHING ELSE.
WHEN I DO PICTURES, I GO
ALL OUT. I REALLY THINK IT IS
EASIER TO MANAGE MY SEVEN.
YOU CAN'T AFFORD TO HUMOR
EACH ONE OF THEM. THEY HAVE
TO LEARN TO DO THINGS WHEN
THEY ARE TOLD.

Maureen O'Sullivan

I DID QUITE ENJOY THE DAYS
WHEN ONE WENT FOR A BEER AT
ONE'S LOCAL IN PARIS AND WOKE
UP IN CORSICA.

Peter O'Toole

ACTING IS JUST BEING A MAN.
BEING HUMAN. NOT FORCING
IT. SOME MAKE IT THEIR ENTIRE
LIFE. BIG MISTAKE.

Peter O'Toole

THE ONLY EXERCISE I TAKE
IS WALKING BEHIND THE
COFFINS OF FRIENDS WHO TOOK
EXERCISE.

Peter O'Toole

I THINK MY BEING SUCH A
NOMAD LET ME INTO ACTING. I
WAS ALWAYS HAVING TO CREATE
A NEW IMAGE WHENEVER WE
MOVED.

Aidan Quinn

I BELIEVE SOME PEOPLE IN THIS
BUSINESS SUFFER FROM FAME
BECAUSE THEY BEHAVE IN A
FAMOUS FASHION.

Stephen Rea

IF YOU'RE PLAYING A LEAD,
YOU'RE SHAPING THE MOVIE.
WHEN YOU'RE PLAYING A
SUPPORTING ROLE, YOU'VE GOT
ONLY A MOMENT TO MAKE IT
COUNT.

Stephen Rea

THAT'S A FUNNY THING, FAME.
PEOPLE DEFINITELY DO TREAT
YOU DIFFERENTLY. WHEN YOU
BEGIN TO BE SUCCESSFUL, PEOPLE
SAY, 'DON'T GO CHANGING.'
WELL, THAT'S EASY TO SAY, BUT
THE FACT IS, YOU DON'T CHANGE
AT ALL – OTHER PEOPLE DO.

Jonathan Rhys Meyers

ACTING IS ONE OF THESE THINGS
THAT I CAN'T REALLY DESCRIBE –
IT'S JUST LIKE, WHY DO YOU LOVE
YOUR MUM AND DAD? YOU KNOW,
YOU JUST DO.

Saoirse Ronan

I WANT TO BE CERTAIN THAT
WHEN I ARRIVE AT DEATH, I'M
TOTALLY EXHAUSTED.

Fiona Shaw

WHAT'S LOVELY ABOUT WHAT
I DO FOR A LIVING IS THE
VAST CHASM OF VARIETY THAT
CONSTANTLY JUST COMES AT YOU
FROM
ALL ANGLES.

Robert Sheehan

In New York we used to get great reviews, and then we'd come back to Ireland and it would be 'populist', 'rural', culchie, whatever derogatory term they could throw at us.

Pat Shortt

I THINK THAT 'THEATRE OF RELATIONSHIP' IS BECOMING POPULAR AGAIN, APPARENTLY AS A RESULT OF REALITY TELEVISION. WERE FASCINATED BY THE WAY PEOPLE BEHAVE – THAT'S WHAT THEATRE'S ALWAYS BEEN ABOUT, THE INVESTIGATION OF PEOPLE AND HUMAN BEHAVIOUR.

Alan Stanford

MOST OF THE MATERIAL IS MY
OWN, STOLEN FROM THE PLAIN
PEOPLE OF IRELAND, RE-SPRAYED,
RE-MOULDED, RE-BORED AND
GIVEN FALSE NUMBER PLATES.

Niall Tóibín

I WAS REALLY INTO FILMS WHEN
I WAS YOUNGER, BUT I FEEL LIKE
A BIT OF A PHONY SOMETIMES
- I STARTED ACTING BECAUSE
I DIDN'T KNOW WHAT ELSE
TO DO. I FILLED IN ALL THESE
UNIVERSITY APPLICATION FORMS
AND HONESTLY DIDN'T WANT TO
DO ANY OF THE COURSES.

Aidan Turner

INDEX